AF091784

# This Notebook Belongs To

____________________________________

Copyright © 2019 RWG

All rights reserved.

www.ingramcontent.com/pod-product-compliance
Lightning Source LLC
LaVergne TN
LVHW060209080526
838202LV00052B/4218
* 9 7 8 5 5 7 6 7 6 9 4 7 6 *